Best of the West Biographies

Wyatt Earp

Wild West Lawman

Elaine Landau

Enslow Publishers, Inc.

40 Industrial Road   PO Box 38
Box 398   Aldershot
Berkeley Heights, NJ 07922   Hants GU12 6BP
USA   UK

http://www.enslow.com

Library of Congress Cataloging-in-Publication Data

Landau, Elaine.
 Wyatt Earp : wild west lawman / Elaine Landau.
   p. cm. — (Best of the West biographies)
 Summary: A biography of the lawman who helped to bring order to "The Wickedest Town in the West," Dodge City, Kansas.
 Includes bibliographical references and index.
 ISBN 0-7660-2217-X (hardcover)
 1. Earp, Wyatt, 1848–1929—Juvenile literature. 2. Peace officers—Southwest, New—Biography—Juvenile literature. 3. Southwest, New—Biography—Juvenile literature. 4. Dodge City (Kan.)—History—19th century—Juvenile literature. 5. Tombstone (Ariz.)—History—19th century—Juvenile literature. [1. Earp, Wyatt, 1848-1929. 2. Peace officers.] I. Title. II. Series.
 F786.E18L36 2004
 978'.02'092—dc21

                                 2003010336

Printed in the United States of America

10 9 8 7 6 5 4 3 2 1

To Our Readers: We have done our best to make sure that all Internet addresses in this book were active and appropriate when we went to press. However, the author and publisher have no control over and assume no liability for the material available on those Internet sites or on other Web sites they may link to. Any comments or suggestions can be sent by e-mail to comments@enslow.com or to the address on the back cover.

Illustration Credits: Arizona Historical Society Library, pp. 30, 35; © 1999 Artville, Inc., p. 23; © Corel Corporation, pp. 1, 2-3, 5, 6, 8, 10, 11 (background), 16, 18, 20, 28, 39; Denver Public Library, Western History Department, p. 43; Enslow Publishers, Inc., p. 37; Courtesy Mercaldo Archives, reproduced from the *Dictionary of American Portraits*, published by Dover Publications, Inc., in 1967, pp. 4, 24, 29, 32; National Archives and Records Administration, p. 26; Photos.com, pp. 11, 12, 36; Reproduced from the Collections of the Library of Congress, pp. 14, 21, 40;

Cover Illustration: © Corel Corporation (background); Courtesy Mercaldo Archives, reproduced from the *Dictionary of American Portraits*, published by Dover Publications, Inc., in 1967 (Wyatt Earp).

Contents

Wyatt Earp was one of the most famous lawmen of the Wild West.

Welcome to Dodge

In 1876, Dodge City, Kansas, was known as "The Wickedest Town in the West." That was no lie. It was a rough and lawless place. Dodge City was a cowtown. It was where cattle were sold and cowboys were paid.

These cowboys had worked hard for months on cattle drives. Dodge was the last stop on the trail. Now they drank hard in the city's many saloons. Liquor flowed easily in Dodge. Saloons were open twenty-four hours a day. There was no shortage of gambling casinos, either. The same was true for dancehall girls. They were there to entertain the cowboys.

Dodge City also had its share of gamblers and outlaws. Often, the young cowboys were no match for these men. Fights and brawls were common. Sometimes, fistfights turned into gunfights. Bullets replaced words. People in Dodge became used to the sound of gunfire after dark. One newspaper reporter described the town this way: "Horse thieves, burglars, peace disturbers and even murderers go at large."

In time, Dodge City would be tamed. Until then, a team of lawmen tried to control things. These men had their work cut out for them. Dodge's assistant marshal stood out from the rest. He was a tall, slender, blondish man.

After a hard day's work, cowboys would celebrate the night in Dodge City.

Some said his piercing blue eyes could look straight through a criminal.

This man took his job seriously. As an assistant marshal in a tough town, he had to be serious. He never joked and rarely smiled. His name was Wyatt Earp.

Wyatt Earp had a kind of quiet strength. He knew how to shoot, but he did not rely on that skill. After Earp came to Dodge City, shootings by law officers greatly lessened.

But Wyatt Earp did not hide from danger. He used his gun in another way. He often hit wrongdoers over the head with the butt of his gun. This was known as "buffaloing." It sometimes left a nasty gash. But in the long run, it saved lives. That was the goal. Cowtowns wanted their customers controlled, not killed.

Many people admired Wyatt Earp. He has been praised as an outstanding lawman. Yet, others thought far less of him. That was because there were also unsettling rumors about Earp. Some say he broke the law as often as he upheld it. What is the truth about Wyatt Earp? Was he a hero or a villain?

At the Start

Wyatt Earp became famous in the Wild West. But he did not start out there. Wyatt was born in Monmouth, Illinois, on March 19, 1848. He came from a large family. Wyatt's parents, Nicholas and Virginia Earp, had eight children. There were five boys and three girls. Wyatt also had a half-brother from his father's first marriage.

Wyatt's father had many different jobs. During his life, Nicholas Earp worked as a farmer, storekeeper, lawman, soldier, and judge. He held other jobs, as well. That meant that the family often moved.

Wyatt became used to living in new places. He never stayed at one school very long, yet he

still learned to read and write. Moving around also made it hard to have friends. So the Earp brothers became especially close. As children, they always looked out for one another. This continued as they grew older.

In 1861, the Civil War broke out. Wyatt's father joined the Union Army. So did Wyatt's half-brother, Newton, and his older brothers, James and Virgil. Thirteen-year-old Wyatt ached to go to war. The boy felt that soldiering was in his blood. His full name was Wyatt Berry Stapp Earp. He had been named after his father's commander in the Mexican-American War.

Now Wyatt felt it was his turn to serve. But his father felt differently. He said that Wyatt was too young. The boy refused to listen. Wyatt ran off and joined up with some soldiers anyway. To his disappointment, his father was among them. Wyatt was promptly sent home.

While others fought, Wyatt farmed. For the next three years, he raised corn crops. His younger brothers, Warren and Morgan, helped.

American Indians would sometimes attack wagon trains. They felt the settlers were imposing on the land they had lived on for years.

But that did not change things. Wyatt hated farming. He longed for a more exciting life.

Things became more exciting for Wyatt after the war. In 1864, Nicholas Earp moved his family once again. This time, they headed for California. The Earps bought two covered wagons for the trip. They joined a small wagon train of about forty other families.

Wyatt was extremely helpful during the

A Question of Honesty

In Lamar, Missouri, Wyatt Earp had been accused of stealing. But in Wichita, Kansas, he became well known for his honesty. Once, Wyatt locked up a drunken cowboy overnight. The cowboy had $500 on him. When the young man awoke the next morning, he remembered very little. He would not have known what had happened to his money. Yet Wyatt returned every dollar. This was unusual. A lot of cowtown lawmen would have kept the money.

The newspapers praised Wyatt for it. A newspaper called *The Beacon* said, "There are but few other places where the $500 roll would have ever been heard from."

During Wyatt Earp's time, most men carried guns in the Wild West.

seven-month journey. Despite being only sixteen, he did a man's work. Wyatt drove one of the wagons. During the rest stops, he hunted and fished. That brought in more food. Twice he helped fight off American Indian raids, too.

In a way, Wyatt grew up on that trip. Nicholas Earp had wanted his son to study law in California. But now Wyatt did what he wanted. His brother Virgil got a job driving freight wagons. Wyatt worked with him, helping to unload the freight. He also drove the wagon for short distances.

The work was not easy. The route went through both mountain passes and stretches of desert. At times, there were outlaws to deal with. But that never stopped the Earp brothers. Wyatt and Virgil were a strong team. They knew they could count on each other.

Wyatt loved the rough-and-tumble West. Like his father, he would always have an urge to roam. But after a while, much of his family moved back to back to Missouri. This time, Nicholas Earp bought a farm in a town called Lamar. In 1869, Wyatt joined them there. By then, he had fulfilled his contract with the freight company.

Wyatt Earp tried to settle down in Lamar. He fell in love with a young girl named Urilla Sutherland. She was the daughter of a local hotel owner. The couple married on January 3, 1870. Earp was twenty-two at the time. The bride was just seventeen. Two months later, Earp got his first job as a lawman. He was elected constable of Lamar. It would be the only time Wyatt Earp ever ran for office.

Gunfights were the way disagreements were often settled in the Wild West.

It should have been the best of times for Wyatt Earp. Unfortunately, it was not. His wife died within the year. Not much is known about her death. Some said she died of the disease typhus. Others said she died in childbirth.

In any case, Urilla's family blamed Wyatt Earp for her death. The reason for this is also not clear. It may be because they felt Urilla had been too young to marry at all. The bad feelings

erupted in a street fight between Urilla's brothers and the Earp boys.

In 1871, Wyatt Earp faced other problems, as well. He was said to have misused his position as constable. Earp was accused of stealing money. It is not known whether the charges were true. Wyatt Earp left town before the case went to court. He never returned to Lamar.

Earp went to eastern Oklahoma. But he met with trouble there, too. On March 28, 1871, Wyatt Earp and two other men were arrested for horse stealing. It did not look good for Earp. However, one of the other men was tried first. He was found not guilty. After that, the law lost interest in the case. Wyatt Earp was set free.

Was Wyatt Earp innocent or guilty? Once again, the facts were never made clear. Earp was just twenty-three years old. Yet he had already been in trouble twice. It was a shaky beginning. Few would have guessed that Wyatt Earp would later be known for his outstanding police work.

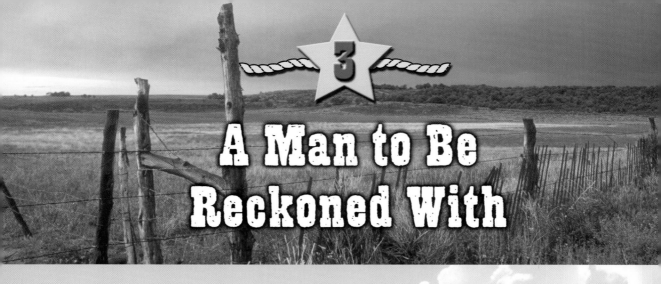

A Man to Be Reckoned With

After leaving Oklahoma, Wyatt Earp had many jobs. These often took him to new places. For a while, he was a buffalo hunter. Earp was also a government land surveyor. On this job, he mapped out new territory.

In 1873, Wyatt Earp found himself in Ellsworth, Kansas. Ellsworth was one of many Western cowtowns. Lawmen there often had to deal with drunken and disorderly cowboys.

The real trouble in Ellsworth began when the sheriff was shot. He was killed by a shady cowboy named Billy Thompson. After the shooting, Thompson needed to get out of town quickly. His brother, Ben, decided to help. So did some of their friends. They drew their guns to cover Thompson as he escaped.

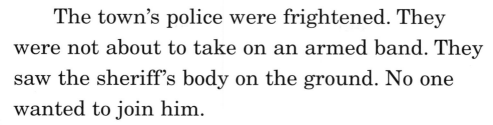
The town's police were frightened. They were not about to take on an armed band. They saw the sheriff's body on the ground. No one wanted to join him.

Ellsworth's mayor was furious. He fired the whole police force on the spot. Some say that was when Wyatt Earp came to the rescue. He offered to help, and the mayor eagerly accepted. He pinned a badge on Earp and let him take over.

Wyatt Earp strapped on a pair of six-shooters. He slowly walked up to Ben Thompson and told him that he had a choice. He could either be arrested or killed. Ben Thompson put down his gun. He did not want to die. His friends followed his lead. Wyatt Earp took Thompson to jail without having to fire a single shot.

After that, Wyatt Earp was a hero. Ben Thompson later stood trial. However, the judge's ruling upset Earp. Thompson only had to pay a twenty-dollar fine. Wyatt felt that the town did not value its lawmen. He gave back the badge. Ellsworth would have to find someone else to protect it.

Did things really happen that way in Ellsworth? No one can be sure. Wyatt Earp's name is not mentioned in the court records. Yet the story has often been repeated through the years.

Next, Wyatt Earp served as deputy marshal in Wichita, Kansas. Earp moved there from

A game called Faro was often played in the saloons of the Wild West. This painting, titled "Faro Layout in Mint Saloon," was painted by Olaf C. Seltzer.

Ellsworth in 1874. Wichita was another cowtown that needed taming. Things were never quiet there. People yelled and cursed in the streets. Drunken cowboys often shot off their guns in the street.

People in Wichita already knew of Wyatt Earp. They had heard how he handled Ben Thompson in Ellsworth. Wyatt's fame as a lawman grew even greater in Wichita. People felt that he was strict but fair. At times, he faced some very dangerous outlaws. Yet he kept the peace without killing a single man. Years after Wyatt Earp left Wichita, people still spoke of his daring. One police chief would say, "He was the most fearless man I ever saw."

Wyatt Earp enjoyed all the praise. However, he had some embarrassing moments, too. Wyatt was in a saloon one night when his gun fell out of its holster. The weapon hit a chair and fired. The bullet went straight through Wyatt Earp's coattail. Luckily, he was not hurt. But that was the closest he ever came to shooting a man in Wichita. He nearly caught his own bullet!

Taming Dodge

After Wichita, Wyatt Earp went to Dodge City. He arrived in the spring of 1876 to serve as assistant marshal. In Dodge, Earp worked under Marshal Larry Deger. Deger was a big man. He weighed over three hundred pounds. He was not very active. Instead, he spent most of the day doing paperwork.

The town counted on Wyatt Earp to keep the peace. That was a tall order. People liked to make their own rules in Dodge. It was a dangerous place.

Nevertheless, Wyatt Earp did his best. He started by picking his own deputies. Earp's brother Morgan was already a Dodge City deputy. That was very helpful. But he also

chose Bat Masterson and two of Masterson's brothers. Earp had met Masterson when he was a government surveyor. The men liked and trusted one another. Bat Masterson was already known as a brave fighter. Earp felt he would be a good man to have on the force. Taming Dodge would not be easy.

Guns had been banned in Dodge City. Only lawmen could carry arms. Everyone else had to check their weapons at the stores, saloons, or hotels. Wyatt Earp and his men had to enforce this rule. That was sometimes risky.

But Wyatt Earp usually succeeded. He often talked rowdy cowboys into laying

Wyatt Earp was feared by the outlaws of Dodge City.

down their weapons. When talking did not work, Earp used buffaloing. Wyatt Earp was also an excellent boxer. At times, his fists stopped troublemakers. Wyatt Earp demanded respect—and he got it.

By October 1876, Dodge City had calmed down. The cowboys had gone back to their Texas ranches. They would not return before the next cattle drive. Wyatt Earp was ready to leave Dodge, too. As always, he felt the need to roam the country.

This time, he headed for North Dakota's Black Hills. He took his brother Morgan with him. Gold had been found there. Wyatt Earp hoped to become rich.

Wyatt and Morgan Earp went to Deadwood City. Some of the richest strikes had come from that area. But the Earp brothers were too late. By then, the best claims had already been taken. No one was becoming wealthy in Deadwood anymore.

To make things worse, winter had started to set in. It had gotten cold and there was

Wyatt Earp helped rid Dodge City, Kansas, of crime. He would later go on to make a name for himself in Tombstone, Arizona.

already snow on the ground. Deadwood no longer seemed very promising. Morgan Earp went back to Dodge. Wyatt Earp stayed and sold firewood to the miners. It was hard work, but he made sure he was paid well for it.

Wyatt Earp had other jobs, too. He was an armed guard on the Wells Fargo stagecoaches leaving Deadwood. This was known as "riding shotgun." These stagecoaches carried large amounts of gold. At times, they were attacked by robbers. But Wyatt Earp was used to danger. He would shoot at the outlaws to scare them off. He never lost a shipment or killed a man.

Wyatt Earp also worked as a bounty hunter. He brought outlaws to justice for the reward money. While on the run, these criminals often covered a lot of ground. Earp's manhunts did, too. One chase took Wyatt through Oklahoma and Texas.

During this time, Wyatt Earp met many people. One of them became his best friend. He was a dentist named Dr. John Henry Holliday. Holliday was not what you would expect in a dentist. He

Doc Holliday had a good sense of humor and was a very quick shot.

spent most of his time gambling and drinking. He was also said to be ruthless and mean-tempered. Yet "Doc" Holliday admired Earp. He remained loyal to him through the years.

Chasing outlaws kept Wyatt Earp busy for months. Meanwhile, back in Dodge, trouble had been brewing. Earp received a telegram asking him to return. He did so in the spring of 1878. Soon after, Doc Holliday followed him to Kansas. By then, Dodge was a city out of control.

Ed Masterson was one of Bat's brothers. He had taken over as Dodge's marshal, but was not in the job for long. On the evening of April 9, 1878, Ed Masterson was shot by a drunken cowboy. The cowboy put a bullet in the marshal's stomach. He had fired at close range. The flash from the gun had even set Masterson's shirt on fire. The marshal died soon afterward.

Wyatt Earp knew that he had to end the killing. So he came up with a plan. He would stop trouble before it started. Cowboys toting

This photo of the Dodge City "Peace Commissioners" was taken in 1890. Pictured are, from left to right, Chas. Basset, W.H. Harris, Wyatt Earp, Luke Short, L. McLean, Bat Masterson, and Neal Brown.

guns were immediately taken to jail. Disorderly behavior also meant a night in jail. Earp received a salary. He was paid another dollar for every arrest made. Before long, he earned a tidy sum. Dodge became much calmer, as well.

Before returning to Dodge, Wyatt Earp had never killed a man. But that would change. One night in July 1878, Earp, Doc Holliday, Bat Masterson, and some other friends were at a Dodge music hall. They were enjoying the show when suddenly they heard gunfire. Three men on horseback were outside. They had begun shooting into the music hall.

Doc Holliday quickly dropped to the floor. He did not want to be hit. Bat Masterson did the same. But Wyatt Earp and another man ran outside to stop the shooters. They fired at the men as they rode away. Earp hit one of them. He was a man named George Hoy. Hoy died several weeks later.

No one was sure why the men had shot up the music hall. Earp thought that Hoy had been hired to do it. He believed that some powerful men in Dodge wanted him dead. However, this was never proven.

George Hoy was the first man Wyatt Earp ever killed. He would not be the last.

Tombstone

By September 1879, things were quieter in Dodge. Wyatt Earp was ready for a change. His brother Virgil now lived in Arizona. Silver had been discovered there. Wyatt Earp had not been successful looking for gold. He thought he might do better in silver mining. He also thought about starting a stagecoach line there.

Earp packed up and headed for Tombstone, a mining camp in Pima County, Arizona. His brothers James and Morgan came along, too. Doc Holliday later joined them there, as well.

None of the Earps became rich in the silver mines. Wyatt Earp never began the stagecoach line, either. But before long, they found other work. James became a bartender while Wyatt and Morgan Earp rode shotgun on Wells Fargo stagecoaches. Wyatt Earp also worked as a dealer in the gambling houses. Virgil Earp took over the job as deputy city marshal after the old marshal was killed.

However, not everyone in Tombstone made an honest living. It was also home to an outlaw gang. These men were cattle thieves. They robbed stagecoaches, too. The gang was known as the "Cowboys."

The "Cowboys" usually rode into Mexico to steal cattle. They brought the stolen herds back to Tombstone. There, the cattle's brand was changed and the cows were sold.

Virgil Earp respected the law and became deputy city marshal of Tombstone.

Among the worst of the "Cowboys" were the Clantons. There was Old Man Clanton and his sons, Ike, Phineas, and Billy. The Clantons worked closely with two brothers, Frank and Tom McLaury. They would bring their stolen cattle to the McLaurys' ranch. The McLaurys

The McLaury brothers, Tom (left) and Frank (right), were members of the infamous "Cowboys."

changed the cattle's brand. They also sold the cows for the Clantons. "Curly Bill" Brocius and Frank Stilwell were two other troublesome "Cowboys." They often broke the law for their own gain, as well.

These cattle thieves did not just steal cows in Mexico. In the summer of 1880, they took six mules from Camp Rucker, a U.S. army camp. As a lawman, Virgil Earp helped with the case. A search party was formed to find the missing animals. Virgil made Wyatt and Morgan Earp deputies. They joined the search party, too.

Virgil Earp soon learned the truth. "Curly Bill" Brocius and the McLaurys were among the cattle thieves he was after. They had tried to change the army brand of "US" to "D8." Nevertheless, both denied having anything to do with it. The McLaurys were especially angry at Virgil Earp for accusing them. That was the start of bad feelings between the Earps and the "Cowboys."

At times, the "Cowboys" baited the Earps. Eighteen-year-old Billy Clanton stole one of

Wyatt Earp's horses. It was a prize-winning racehorse. Earp learned where the horse was. He and Doc Holliday rode out to get it. Clanton gave the horse back without a fight. He threatened to steal it again, though.

During this time, Morgan Earp had remained a deputy. He helped Virgil Earp keep the peace. At times, Wyatt Earp helped, too. He served as a special officer when needed. He took over if Virgil Earp was out of town.

The Earp brothers were kept busy in Tombstone. Virgil and Morgan Earp chased horse thieves and stagecoach robbers. If an extra man was needed, they called on Wyatt Earp. Often, the

Morgan Earp helped Virgil keep the peace in Tombstone.

Earps broke up fights. Nevertheless, there were still some shoot-outs. Usually, the "Cowboys" were behind the trouble.

Finally, on the night of October 25, 1881, things reached a boiling point. Ike Clanton and Tom McLaury rode into town to drink and gamble. By midnight, Clanton was very drunk.

Doc Holliday was at the same saloon. He had also had too much to drink. Wyatt and Morgan Earp were there, too. Holliday and Clanton began to argue and threaten one another.

It looked like there might be a fight. So the men moved their argument outside. Morgan and Wyatt Earp followed them. Hearing the noise, Virgil Earp came out of a nearby saloon, too. Virgil Earp separated the men. He said he would arrest them if they did not stop arguing. He hoped that would be the end of it.

Ike Clanton should have gone home. Instead, he went to another saloon. He played poker there until six in the morning. After the card game, he started drinking again. Now he threatened to kill Doc Holliday and the Earps.

Virgil Earp thought that Ike Clanton could be dangerous. So he, along with Wyatt and Morgan Earp, went to arrest him. The men "buffaloed" Clanton and took his gun. They brought him directly to court. The judge fined Ike Clanton for carrying a weapon in town. However, once he paid the money, Clanton was set free.

Ike Clanton and Tom McLaury remained in town. Although he no longer had a gun, Clanton still threatened the Earps. Some of the townspeople heard him. They warned Wyatt Earp and his brothers.

The Earps had reason to worry. Ike Clanton and Tom McLaury were soon joined by their brothers, Billy Clanton and Frank McLaury. Frank McLaury was the best shot for miles. The men went to the gun store and bought ammunition. Ike Clanton tried to buy another gun, but had no luck. The gun shop owner saw that he was drunk. He refused to sell him one.

Ike Clanton often drank too much alcohol and got himself into trouble.

Virgil Earp was the city marshal. But there was another lawman in Tombstone that day. It was Sheriff Johnny Behan. Behan was the county sheriff. His job was to patrol the area outside Tombstone's city limits. Behan had always liked the "Cowboys" better than the Earps. There had been some jealousy between him and Wyatt Earp. Behan's girlfriend, Josie Marcus, had left him for Wyatt Earp. Earp had almost gotten his job, as well.

But now Behan saw trouble coming. He just wanted to keep the peace. Sheriff Behan asked

The Earps and Holliday walked down a dusty street to face the "Cowboys."

both the Clantons and the McLaurys to give up their guns. They replied that the Earps had to give up theirs first.

That was not going to happen. Instead, Wyatt Earp and his brothers prepared for a showdown. By noon, Wyatt, Virgil, and Morgan Earp had met Doc Holliday in the street. Both Wyatt Earp and Doc Holliday were acting as special officers or deputies that day.

The "Cowboys" had walked to an empty lot near the O.K. Corral. The Earps and Doc Holliday were ready to face them as lawmen. They wanted to take the guns from the

"Cowboys." As they walked toward the O.K. Corral, they met Johnny Behan. Behan ordered them to go back. He promised to disarm the "Cowboys" himself.

But it was too late for that. Doc Holliday and the Earps kept walking. Finally, they were face-to-face with the "Cowboys." Virgil Earp ordered them to put down their weapons. Billy Clanton and Frank McLaury cocked their pistols, instead. Virgil Earp thought they were going to shoot.

Seconds later, shots rang out. Bullets

The gunfight at the O.K. Corral was quick and very deadly.

from both sides flew through the air. The shooting was over in about thirty seconds. By then, Frank McLaury was dead on the sidewalk. Billy Clanton and Tom McLaury died later, as well. Virgil and Morgan Earp were wounded. Doc Holliday was also hurt. Only Wyatt Earp was unharmed. He left the gunfight without a scratch.

Ike Clanton had started the trouble that day. But before the shooting started, he ran away. Sheriff Behan had quickly headed for cover, as well.

Some people in town sided with the Earps. They said that the men were just doing their job. They had only fired to defend themselves. Others said the "Cowboys" had been wronged. The gunfight at O.K. Corral became famous. People would argue about who was at fault for over a century. Some praised Wyatt Earp's bravery. Others called him a murderer.

Ike Clanton loudly accused the Earps of murder. They stood trial along with Doc Holliday. The judge found them not guilty. As expected, the "Cowboys" were not pleased. Now more than ever, they wanted blood.

None of the Earps were safe anymore. Virgil Earp was the first to feel the anger of the "Cowboys." It happened one night while he was out on patrol. Shots rang out in the darkness. Virgil Earp was hit, but he survived. No one saw the gunman. However, Ike Clanton's hat was found nearby.

Clanton was tried for the crime. But he did not go to prison. He had his friends lie in court. They swore that he was not in Tombstone when it happened. Now it was Wyatt Earp's turn to be angry. He felt that he could not trust the law.

Unfortunately, the "Cowboys" were still not finished. On March 18, 1882, Wyatt and Morgan Earp were playing pool at a saloon. Suddenly, the saloon doors flung open and there was gunfire. Several men began shooting at the Earps. A bullet whisked right past Wyatt Earp's head. Morgan Earp was not as lucky. Another

Playing pool was a favorite pastime in the Old West. Morgan Earp was playing pool when he was shot to death.

bullet killed him. The shooters made a speedy getaway.

It all happened very quickly. Wyatt Earp did not see who had fired the shots. Nevertheless, he vowed to find his brother's killers. This time he would not bring them in. He would take care of things his own way.

Wyatt Earp got a small group of friends together to ride with. He learned that three men were involved in his brother's murder. Earp tracked them down. Some say that at least one of the men had begged for his life. Yet Wyatt Earp did not rest until all three were dead.

The killings were reported in local newspapers. Wyatt Earp's hunt for his brother's murderers became known as the Vendetta Drive. Some people said that Earp only wanted justice. Many more saw him as a good lawman who had gone bad.

Wyatt Earp was now a wanted criminal. For a time, Sheriff Johnny Behan was determined to arrest him. But catching Wyatt

Earp was not easy. He quickly left Tombstone and never returned. Afterward he kept moving. Earp was spotted in different parts of New Mexico, Colorado, Idaho, and California.

At first, Earp was seen with Doc Holliday. Later he traveled with Josie, the woman who had once been with Johnny Behan. After a while, they married.

Now Wyatt Earp worked as a dealer in gambling houses. He also tried mining again. In 1896, Wyatt and Josie Earp went to Nome, Alaska. They opened a very successful saloon there. The couple made a good deal of money.

Unfortunately, they did not keep it very long. Both Wyatt and Josie Earp lost a lot of money gambling. They also made some bad investments.

In time, the charges against Wyatt Earp were dropped. The law had stopped looking for him. However, in 1928, a writer named Stuart Lake found Earp. Lake wrote a book about Earp called *Frontier Marshal*. In it, he described Wyatt Earp as a great hero.

Hollywood liked that view of him. There were movies and TV shows about Wyatt Earp. In them, he was always "brave, courageous, and bold."

The real Wyatt Earp died on January 13, 1929. He was eighty-one years old. During his life, he had chased outlaws and had been chased himself. Yet a bullet did not kill Wyatt Earp. He did not die on the run, or at the end of a rope. Wyatt Earp died peacefully in bed. He was a man who had done both good and bad on the Western frontier. He is someone who is not likely to be forgotten.

Wyatt Earp was eighty years old when this picture was taken.

Timeline

1848—Wyatt Berry Stapp Earp is born on March 19.

1864—The Earp family moves to California.

1869—Wyatt Earp moves to Lamar, Missouri.

1870—Wyatt Earp marries Urilla Sutherland on January 3. In March, Wyatt is elected constable of Lamar.

1871—Wyatt Earp is accused of stealing money in Lamar and horses in eastern Oklahoma.

1873—Wyatt Earp becomes a lawman in Ellsworth, Kansas.

1876—In the spring, Wyatt Earp becomes assistant marshal in Dodge City, Kansas. He leaves Dodge in October of that year.

1878—Wyatt Earp returns to Dodge City.

1879—Wyatt Earp arrives in Tombstone, Arizona.

1881—The famous gunfight at the O.K. Corral takes place on October 26.

1929—Wyatt Earp dies on January 13.

Words to Know

ammunition—Objects, such as bullets, that can be fired from weapons.

bluff—Pretending to be in a better position than you really are.

buffaloing—Hitting someone over the head with the butt of a gun.

constable—A law officer responsible for keeping the peace in a town.

deputy—A person who assists a law officer with his or her duties.

gambling—To bet money on the end result of a race or game.

land surveyor—Someone who maps out new areas.

marshal—A city law officer.

special officer—Someone who is temporarily made a law officer for a special purpose.

telegram—A message sent by telegraph.

Reading About Wyatt Earp

Collins, James L. *Settling the American West*. Danbury, Conn.: Franklin Watts, 1993.

Hicks, Peter. *You Wouldn't Want to Live in a Wild West Town*. Danbury, Conn.: Franklin Watts, 2002.

Marvis, B. *Bat Masterson: Legends of the West*. Broomall, Penn.: Chelsea House, 2002.

————. *Dodge City: Legends of the West*. Broomall, Penn.: Chelsea House, 2002

Murray, Stuart. *Wild West*. New York: DK Publishing, 2001.

Patent, Dorothy Hindshaw. *Homesteading: Settling America's Heartland*. New York: Walker & Company, 1998.

Roop, Peter and Connie. *Westward Ho, Ho, Ho!* Brookfield, Conn.: Millbrook Press, 1996.

Staeger, Rob. *Wyatt Earp*. Broomall, Penn.: Chelsea House, 2002.

Walker, Paul Robert. *True Tales of the Wild West*. Washington, D.C.: National Geographic, 2002.

Wood, Tim. *The Wild West*. New York: Viking, 1998.

Internet Addresses

Arizona Gunfighters

Experience the drama of the Western frontier at this interesting action Web site.

<http://www.arizonagunfighters.com>

Tombstone Online

This is official site of the Tombstone Chamber of Commerce. It has a great history section.

<http://www.tombstone.org>

Index